FOREWORD

I 'm thrilled to share with you my thoughts on how leaders can empower their people through a commitment to continuous learning.

In the following pages, you will find a strategic roadmap to cultivate a high-performing culture by enabling your people. I blend academic research, real-world examples, and tactical advice to create a holistic model for empowerment. This book provides more than just tips for training - it outlines a comprehensive approach to knowledge sharing, hands-on skill building, coaching, and lifelong development.

The Enablement Skill Stack framework integrates formal training, peer collaboration, targeted development, and managerial mentoring. This multilayered model reflects the complexities of true workplace learning. Enabling your people requires surrounding them with daily opportunities to expand their skills and perspectives.

A key principle woven throughout is empowering self-directed growth while still providing institutional support. People are intrinsically motivated to develop, and savvy leaders tap into that drive. As a lifelong learner myself, I am passionate about fostering agency and ownership over professional journeys.

While these tactics will benefit any organization, they are particularly crucial for teams navigating rapid change or digital disruption. Continuous learning creates the agility and innovation to not just survive but thrive in uncertain times. Investing in your people future-proofs your organization.

This journey requires commitment but offers immense rewards for those who embrace it wholeheartedly. I am honored to be your guide as you cultivate an empowered, future-ready workforce. Approach this book with courage, curiosity, and vision. Onward and upward!

Introduction

I am thrilled to present my new book, *The Enablement Skill Stack Framework*. This is my second book on the topic of enablement, following my previous title, *The Essential Guide to Enablement*.

Enablement continues to be a critical focus for organizations looking to empower their employees and foster a culture of learning. While *The Essential Guide to Enablement* provided a broad overview of enablement strategies, this new book takes a deeper dive into a specific framework I've developed called the Enablement Skill Stack.

Let's get started shaping high impact learning cultures!

CONTENTS

CHAPTER 1 - THE JOURNEY BEGINS

Imagine an organization where employees are highly engaged, turnover is low, and productivity is through the roof. A place filled with motivated people excited to come to work each day. An environment where managers provide coaching and support to help team members continuously expand their skills.

What if I told you that you have the power to create this kind of high-performance culture in your company?

It all starts with establishing the right learning framework. This book will take you step-by-step through implementing the **Enablement Skill Stack** - a strategic model to strengthen your workforce through knowledge and skill building.

WHY CONTINUOUS LEARNING MATTERS

These days, just getting through orientation isn't enough. Top companies keep investing in their employees with regular training, development, and coaching. This culture of continuous learning helps them:

- **Adapt quickly** - new skills empower teams to respond to changes in the market.
  - A software company trains developers on new coding languages so they can build products using the latest technologies.
  - A retailer cross-trains store associates so they can flex between different roles and respond to shifting customer demand.
  - A marketing agency reskills creative teams on new social media platforms and trends as they emerge.
  - A manufacturer trains factory workers on operating new machines and processes so they can adapt manufacturing approaches.

- **Engage employees** - People want to work for companies that care about their growth.
  - An accounting firm covers exam fees and study time for employees pursuing advanced certifications relevant to their development goals.
  - A tech company offers a catalog of online courses employees can use to build skills from coding to management.
  - A healthcare system provides a tuition reimbursement program for nurses pursuing higher degrees.
  - A consulting firm sets aside dedicated time each week for employees to take online training or classes.

- **Boost performance** - Increased abilities drive better outcomes.
  - A call center sees higher customer satisfaction after training agents on rapport building and empathy.
  - A legal firm finds attorneys complete contracts more accurately and quickly after a legal writing workshop.
  - A retail store reports increased sales after training cashiers on product recommendations and upselling.
  - A software company sees fewer engineering bugs and faster release cycles after leveling up developers' coding skills.

- **Future-proof** - Ongoing learning ensures skills stay relevant.
  - A media company trains editorial teams on emerging social media channels and content formats.
  - An car manufacturer trains factory workers on programming and interacting with the newest robotic machinery.
  - A law firm trains attorneys on legal tech applications like e-discovery tools and AI contract review.

When you make enablement part of your company DNA, you gain a real competitive edge. Your enriched workforce is better positioned to meet challenges and seize opportunities.

INTRODUCING THE ENABLEMENT SKILL STACK

The Enablement Skill Stack provides a roadmap to build a high-performing team through four levels of learning:

1. **Foundational Knowledge**

2. **Core Skill Practice**

3. **Targeted Development**

4. **Manager Coaching**

Enablement Skill Stack

Manager Coaching

Targeted Development

Core Skill Practice

Foundational Knowledge

This book will take you through implementing each step. You'll learn from real-world examples and case studies of organizations that uses this model to great success.

Let's get started! The first step on the journey is establishing a learning culture...

The next chapter explores how to lay the groundwork for enablement by modeling lifelong learning as a leader and providing the right resources.

When you support your team's professional growth, you all move forward together. Are you ready to unlock your organization's potential? Let's do this!

BEYOND BOX-CHECKING: A NEW VISION FOR ONBOARDING

The first 90 days in a new role are critical for ramping up new hires. Traditional onboarding programs often follow rigid 30/60/90 day plans to induct employees. However, these dated models can fail to set up long-term success.

Rather than marching through an inventory checklist, the Enablement Skill Stack provides a more strategic vision for onboarding based on elevating ability, not ticking boxes. This people-centered approach fuels ongoing growth.

The Flaws of Prescriptive Timelines

Linear time based (30/60/90 day) plans assume that new employees should grasp certain skills and knowledge by set times. But some pick up proficiency quicker in certain areas while needing more time to master others.

Rigid 30/60/90-day schedules can inadvertently sabotage new hires instead of equipping them for success.

Strict timeline-based plans assume proficiency can be achieved by certain predefined dates. But skills develop at different paces for each person.

Common downsides of dated prescriptive onboarding include:

- **Information Overload**
  Forcing weeks of dense training into a 30-day window is cognitively overwhelming. Effective learning requires time to absorb and practice concepts.
  For example, cramming 50 hours of compliance courses into a month result in shallow retention compared to spacing training over 6 months.

- **Illusion of Expertise**

Checking boxes on training requirements doesn't mean real ability is built. Skills like communication take months of practice to ingrain.

An introvert can complete presenting skills courses without actually becoming comfortable public speaking.

- **Narrow Focus**

Rigid plans often focus only on technical job knowledge, neglecting soft skills like relationship building that are critical for success.

A new sales rep might know the product catalog cold but struggle due to weak client rapport skills.

- **Badge Earning Culture**

Mandatory busywork can encourage box-checking and badge collecting rather than truly learning.

Employees race to complete items like compliance courses as merit badges rather than to enrich themselves.

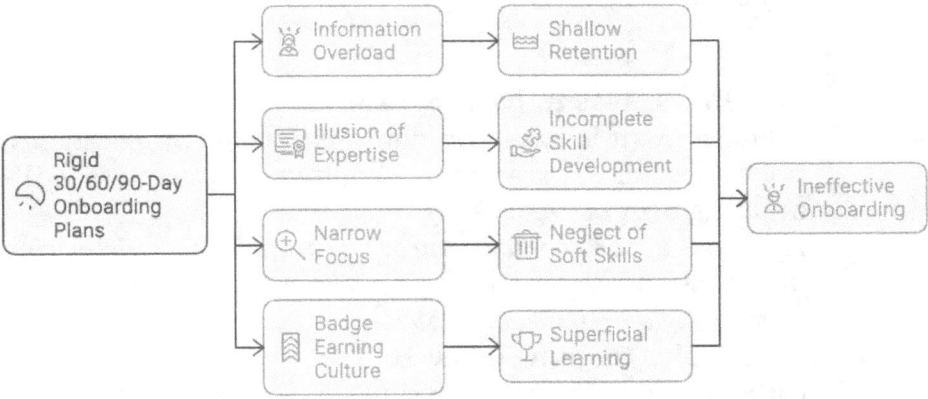

In contrast, the Enablement Skill Stack offers a more personalized, needs-based blueprint for onboarding new hires...

The key is structuring plans around empowering the individual, not adhering to a prescribed checklist. With the Skill Stack approach, crucial abilities are built with intention, resulting in true readiness.

Crafting Customized Enablement Skill Stacks

Rather than a one-size-fits-all blueprint, the Skill Stack approach to onboarding is tailored to each person. This enablement customization:

- **Enables Individualization**

Development plans flex to match knowledge and abilities the learner already possesses, as well as their preferred pace and style of learning.

For example, a marketer coming from a similar role may skip introductory courses to focus on company-specific systems.

- **Drives Goal Orientation**

Milestones map to real proficiencies needed for the role, not just completing generic checklist items. The focus is powering performance.

A project manager's plan will include situational leadership courses to skillfully direct cross-functional teams.

- **Allows Measurable Progress**

Advancement is based on demonstrating competencies, not just clocking seat time. Employees appreciate skill-building over box-checking.

A salesperson must prove proficiency delivering presentations before engaging clients rather than just completing a presentation course.

- **Enables Ongoing Growth**

Onboarding is the starting line, not the finish line. Development continues beyond 90 days through coaching, stretch assignments, and more.

An engineer continues ramping up technical expertise through hands-on complex projects after formal onboarding ends.

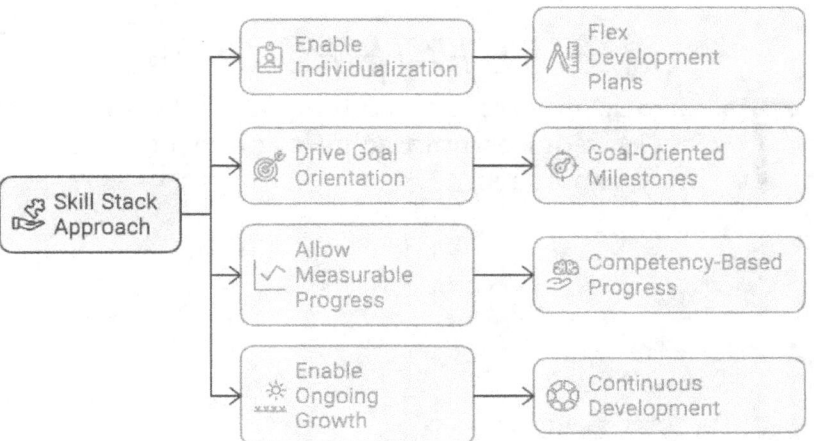

With customized Skill Stacks, new hires master the unique set of abilities needed to excel in their role. The journey is personalized, not prescribed.

THE PATH FORWARD

T ransitioning from dated templated plans to dynamic Skill Stacks requires embracing a more personalized, needs-driven approach:

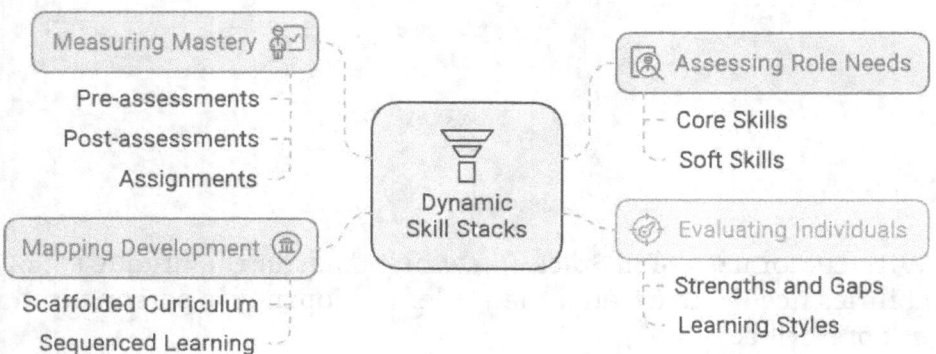

- **Assessing Role Needs**

Analyze each job to identify truly essential knowledge and skills. Look beyond technical abilities to soft skills like communication that enable success.

For an engineer, core skills may include creative problem solving and cross-functional collaboration.

- **Evaluating Individuals**

Through assessments and interviews, determine each new hire's strengths and gaps to customize their plan. Recognize different learning styles.

A salesperson with introvert tendencies may need more practice delivering presentations, while an extrovert focuses on developing listening skills.

- **Mapping Development**

Curate a scaffolded curriculum tailored to the employee that sequences learning for maximum results.

An IT analyst may need technical training first before leadership development makes sense.

- **Measuring Mastery**

Use pre- and post-assessments, assignments, and other techniques to confirm competency - not just participation.

A marketer creates sample social campaigns before launching real initiatives to prove their expertise.

While Skill Stack onboarding requires more upfront needs analysis and customization, it pays off dramatically in empowered, high performing team members equipped for career-long success.

CHAPTER 2 – CREATING A CULTURE OF LEARNING

I n Chapter 1, we explored why continuous learning matters and introduced the Enablement Skill Stack model. Now let's look at how to establish the right environment for enablement.

Embedding learning into your culture starts from the top down. To create change, leaders must role model the behaviors they want to see. When management walks the talk, it sets the tone for the entire company.

Leading by Example:
How Executives Set the Learning Culture

Picture a majestic mountain that team members look to as their guiding north star. This peak represents the executive team - their actions are visible for all and set the tone across the organization.

Like a domino effect, attitudes cascade down from the summit. If leadership shows they value learning, that mindset gets echoed at every level below.

But enabling can't be empty rhetoric. People discern false words from true priorities. Executives must walk the talk through visible, tangible behaviors.

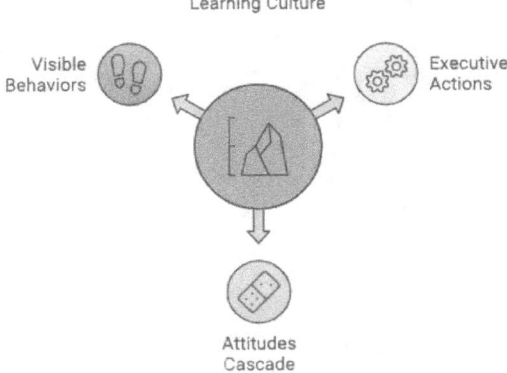

So how can management authentically role model continuous growth?

Hit the Classroom

Enroll in training, from online courses to bootcamps. Leaders should experience being a student to empathize with the learner journey. Stay humble by exposing your own knowledge gaps.

A CEO makes time to take AI and data science courses to stay relevant. His participation signals these skills' importance.

Open Up About Weak Spots

Be transparent about areas where you need to improve. Talk about your development goals. This admission of humanity builds trust and a culture of supportive growth.

The CEO of a major tech firm candidly shares he wants to improve his public speaking skills. This motivates others to identify and vocalize their own growth goals without fear of judgment.

Share Learnings

Discuss insights from books, podcasts, and conferences that ignited new ways of thinking. Ask people to recommend learning resources that enlightened them.

This shows people that leaders are actively growing themselves through self-directed learning. It stimulates knowledge sharing across the organization.

Champion Enablement

Praise managers who proactively develop their teams. Ask about promising enablement initiatives at all-hands meetings. Encourage inclusion of learning objectives in performance reviews.

When executives spotlight professional growth, it gains status as a priority. People recognize enablement as integral to the culture when top management zealously advocates it.

Like the north star steering sailors, leadership illuminates the path forward. Their actions shine light on what matters most. When they embody the growth mindset, the organization ascends together.

Weaving Peer Learning into the Fabric of Work

Picture colleagues gathered in the office cafeteria, not just to eat, but to learn. One team member stands at the front presenting on a topic they specialize in - perhaps a new marketing tactic or engineering process.

Others ask questions and take notes, appreciative to gain insight from their peer's expertise. The presenter shares advice and stories that textbooks can't provide.

This scene depicts just one type of informal peer learning. Beyond formal training, knowledge sharing should become ingrained into the very fabric of how work gets done.

Peer enablement offers benefits traditional structured programs can't provide:

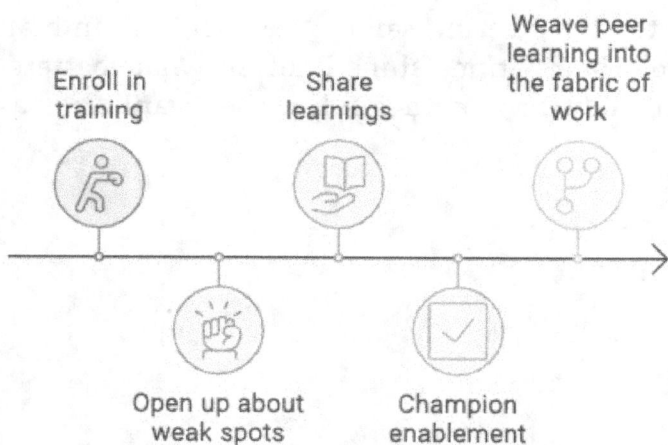

Cultivating a Culture of Continuous Learning and Growth

Authenticity

Employees often best relate to lessons from fellow teammates, not outside experts. The context and trust make knowledge stick.

Cross-pollination

With silos broken down, ideas merge across department borders. Innovation and strategic thinking flourish.

Cost-effectiveness

Informal learning leverages existing human assets for little-to-no expense.

Morale

Serving as a mentor and seeing one's wisdom valued builds pride and engagement.

How can you integrate peer learning into culture? Avenues include:

Lunch and Learns

Colleagues present on their specialties, from Excel tricks to new industry trends.

Job Shadowing

Employees observe different roles to broaden understanding of the business.

Mentorship

Pair junior hires with experienced employees for guidance.

After Action Reviews

Groups reflect on recent project successes and areas to improve.

Like threads woven together into a tapestry, these practices strengthen your enablement fabric. Peer learning serves as a force multiplier to formal training.

Curating a Library to Unlock Self-Directed Learning

The most proactive learners don't just wait for scheduled training - they seek knowledge on their own initiative. Enable self-starters by curating a library with resources aligned to development goals.

This collection of tools for continuous growth arms employees to unlock their potential through self-guided education. Options span:

eLearning Platforms

On-demand courses allow people to learn at their own pace. Cater to different styles with visual, audio, and interactive content.

Books and Audiobooks

Reading expands perspectives and sparks new ways of thinking. Offer titles tailored to your industry and competencies.

Podcasts

Audio shows provide bite-sized learning for commutes or breaks. They suit auditory learners.

Videos

From micro-lessons to documentary style content, video appeals to visual learners.

Online Communities

Forums connect employees to peers beyond company walls to exchange ideas and best practices.

Microlearning

Short daily exercises reinforce knowledge through repetition in small bursts. Gamification boosts engagement.

The library should include both external content and proprietary material such as recorded trainings.

Curation is key - don't just dump random resources. Carefully select materials aligned to skills you aim to build. Curate content for different roles and learning goals.

Empower people to direct their own development journey. The most motivated learners will fully utilize resources made readily available to them.

By demonstrating learning matters and providing tools to unlock growth, the enablement library encourages continuous improvement as a habit. Let the reading commence!

When you make learning part of your culture, engagement soars. Let's continue the journey!

CHAPTER 3 - FOUNDATIONAL KNOWLEDGE

The first step of the Enablement Skill Stack is establishing foundational knowledge. Before employees can excel in their roles, they need a solid grounding in your company's purpose, values, and systems.

This chapter explores what foundational knowledge entails and how to instill it across your organization.

Laying the Knowledge Cornerstone

Imagine an architect designing a skyscraper. Before a single beam can be placed, they must establish a sturdy foundation. Similarly, enabling employees requires laying a knowledge groundwork.

This base provides context, direction, and purpose. Without it, people operate in a void, grasping to understand how their role connects to the broader organization and mission.

Let's explore how to instill this fundamental understanding that serves as a platform for all future learning and growth.

The Cost of a Shaky Foundation

Picture a new hire on their first day, freshly plucked from orientation and placed at their desk. Their manager tosses them a project and rushes off to a meeting. As the new employee turns the pages, their mind floods with questions.

- What are our top business objectives right now?

- How exactly does our product work?

- Who are our major competitors?

- What steps should I take to complete this deliverable?

Lost and overwhelmed, their work suffers as they struggle to find footing.

This scenario demonstrates the cost of not establishing foundational knowledge. Without core understanding, people operate in the dark - not fully grasping company strategy, systems, or context needed to excel.

The Power of Purpose

Now envision that same new team member grounded in foundational knowledge. They fully grasp:

- The organization's purpose, mission, values, and objectives.

- Key roles, responsibilities, and workflows.

- Operational processes and guidelines.

- Compliance requirements and industry landscape.

Armed with this baseline, they can connect daily tasks to the bigger picture. Work is infused with meaning when people see their part in the collective vision.

Foundational knowledge brings confidence, efficiency, and empowerment. Employees feel part of something larger than themselves.

Required Building Blocks

So, what should foundational knowledge cover? Key areas include:

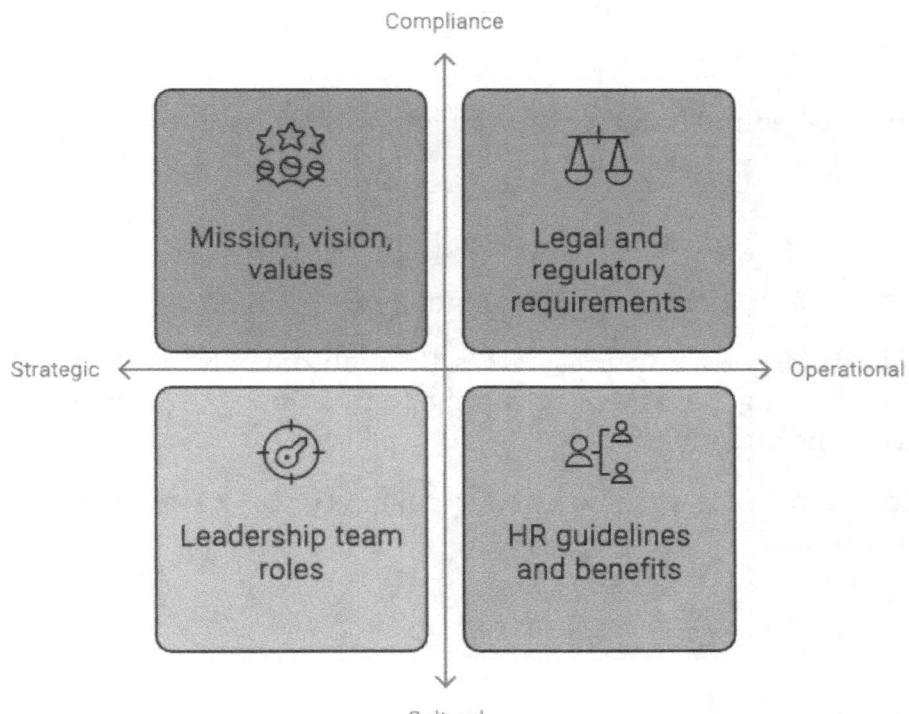

Foundational Knowledge Areas

Company Purpose and Strategy

- Mission, vision, values
- Short and long-term goals
- Competitive landscape

Organizational Structure and Culture

- Leadership team roles
- Department functions

- Cross-collaboration processes

Policies, Procedures, Tools

- HR guidelines and benefits
- Technology systems
- Performance management

Compliance and Industry Knowledge

- Legal and regulatory requirements
- Product development processes
- Quality and safety standards

Solidify expertise in these areas through onboarding, training, and ongoing refreshers. A strong foundation gives employees pride and direction.

Now let's look at how to put foundational knowledge into practice...

BRINGING IT TO LIFE

Onboarding - Immerse new hires in foundational knowledge through activities like:

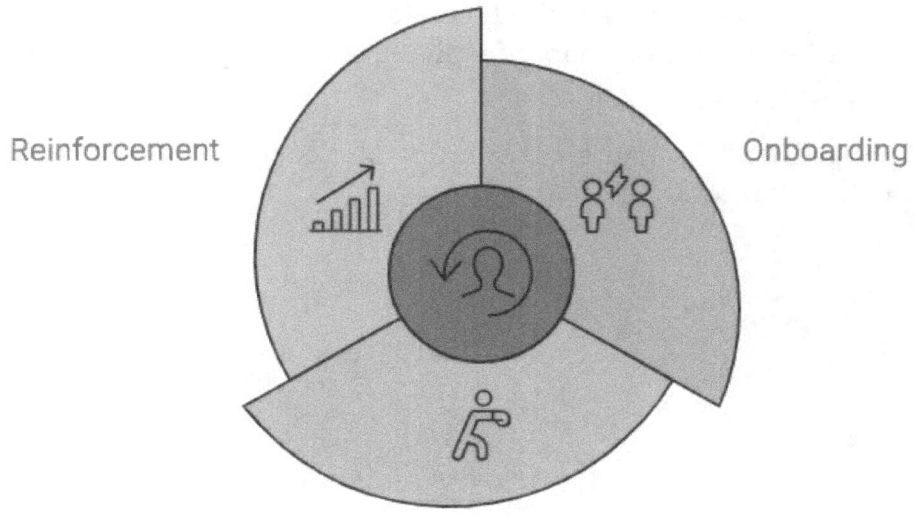

Comprehensive Employee Onboarding

- Interactive presentations
- Facility tours
- Reading material

Training - Offer courses on topics like:

- Company history
- Brand strategy
- Compliance

Reinforcement - Routinely share updates on:

- Goals and initiatives

- Org structure changes

- New policies

Absorbing this information is an ongoing process. Continually reinforce the knowledge that grounds your team in shared purpose.

With this baseline established, employees are ready for the next phase. The upcoming chapter explores core skill practice - where the rubber meets the road.

Equipped with fundamental building blocks, your team can now construct success. Onward!

CHAPTER 4 - CORE SKILL PRACTICE

In the last chapter, we built a knowledge foundation. Now it's time to shift from theory to application through core skill practice.

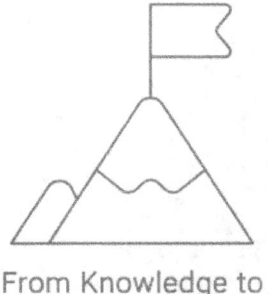

From Knowledge to
Action

Knowing information is one thing, but employees need opportunities to actively apply skills. Core skill practice brings capabilities to life through real-world scenarios.

The Transformative Power of Practice

H ave you heard the old saying, "Practice makes perfect?" This motto rings true not just for athletes and musicians, but equally so at work.

While gaining knowledge through reading and lectures is valuable, active practice cements lessons on a deeper level. As Aristotle said, "For the things we have to learn before we can do them, we learn by doing them."

The Power of Practice in Skill Development

Let's explore why practice is so pivotal for embedding workplace skills:

Confidence Building

Applying skills in low-stakes practice settings allows people to gain self-assurance and poise. Competence grows through experience.

For example, sales reps build confidence by role playing pitches before making high-pressure calls.

Feedback Collection

Attempting new skills provides the chance to observe strengths and areas for improvement firsthand. Constructive feedback helps people refine techniques.

IT help desk reps could practice customer calls and get peer feedback on improving empathy.

Personalized Relevance

Practice enables contextual application, so people learn how skills directly apply to their roles versus generic theory. Relevance boosts retention.

A marketer is more likely to deeply grasp social media skills by practicing posts for their company rather than a fictional business.

Experimentation

A practice sandbox allows employees to test different approaches and styles without real consequences. Creativity thrives through trial and error.

Improvisation games encourage public speaking skills by having people think on their feet and take risks.

Engagement

Being hands-on keeps people active and interested in their own development rather than passive. Immersion sticks better than lectures.

Analyzing real company financials engages finance teams much more than textbook problems.

The brain needs to convert theory into practical mastery. Practice activities make skills second nature through repetition in a supportive environment.

Give your training wings through practice and watch your team soar to new heights.

Methods to Bring Skills to Life Through Practice

Now that we've covered the immense power of practice, let's explore some impactful techniques to build hands-on experiences:

Role Playing

Employees act out fictional scenarios to practice important skills. For example:

- Sales reps conduct mock product pitches to hone persuasion and objection handling.

- Managers role play tense performance reviews to improve delivery of constructive feedback.

- Customer service reps reenact calls with upset clients to build empathy and de-escalation skills.

Colleagues can provide feedback on strengths and areas for improvement after the role play.

Simulations

Immersive computer simulations mimic high-risk situations to allow safe skill practice. Examples include:

- Pilots using flight simulators to refine technical and decision-making abilities.

- Medical students interacting with virtual patients to practice diagnosing conditions.

- Firefighters navigating simulated burning buildings to learn crisis response.

Simulations replicate the intensity of real-world environments with lower stakes.

Apprenticeships

Pair new hires with experienced employees for hands-on mentoring:

- Junior designers are apprenticed to senior creative directors to absorb artistic techniques.

- New accountants are assigned to shadow veteran finance teams to absorb tacit knowledge.

- Entry-level coders are mentored by lead developers to learn industry best practices.

This time-tested practice accelerates onboarding through experiential learning.

Group Workshops

Facilitated sessions with skill-building activities like:

- Improv and public speaking exercises to gain presentation confidence.

- Collaborative design thinking challenges to foster innovation.

- Role rotations in group projects to build cross-functional empathy.

The social format drives engagement through peer interaction.

Driving Lasting Growth

While one-off practice sessions have some benefit, the key to driving lasting growth is making application regular and routine.

Consistency and repetition are powerful in ingraining skills. Just like going to the gym once won't get you fit long-term, periodic practice won't yield lasting gains.

Building frequent opportunities encourages:

Mastery Through Repetition

- Sales reps do weekly role play pitches to continually refine persuasion approaches.

- Managers practice delivering feedback in monthly simulated reviews to build coaching muscles.

- Engineers participate in code collaboration days every 2 weeks to improve skills.

Reinforcement of Lessons

- Customer service reps reflect on support calls after each shift to cement learning.

- Finance teams revisit financial models quarterly to keep analytical skills sharp.

- Marketers offer feedback on each other's social media posts daily to hone content skills.

Progress Benchmarking

- Hospital nurses take clinical skills assessments every 6 months to gauge improvements.

- Software engineers complete technical proficiency tests annually to measure growth.

- Lawyers review video recordings of trial role plays twice a year to see refinements.

Weave practice into weekly, monthly, quarterly, and annual rhythms relevant to each role. Consistency compounds abilities exponentially over time.

Also provide resources like playbooks and tip sheets to enable self-practice.

Ongoing application cements skills at a deeply ingrained level. Let's keep building on this strong foundation through targeted development!

CHAPTER 5 - TARGETED DEVELOPMENT

W e've established a solid foundation and provided opportunities for hands-on skill practice. Now it's time for targeted development to build specific competencies.

While broad training on universal topics has benefits, personalized learning tailored to specific needs has proven more impactful.

Targeted development strategically aligns training to everyone's strengths, weaknesses, and professional goals as well as the organization's business objectives.

This precision enables efficient, high-ROI enablement by addressing the right skills gaps for the right people at the right time. Like a laser focus, targeted training concentrates energy and resources for maximum results.

Getting Specific

Targeted development involves getting granular about:

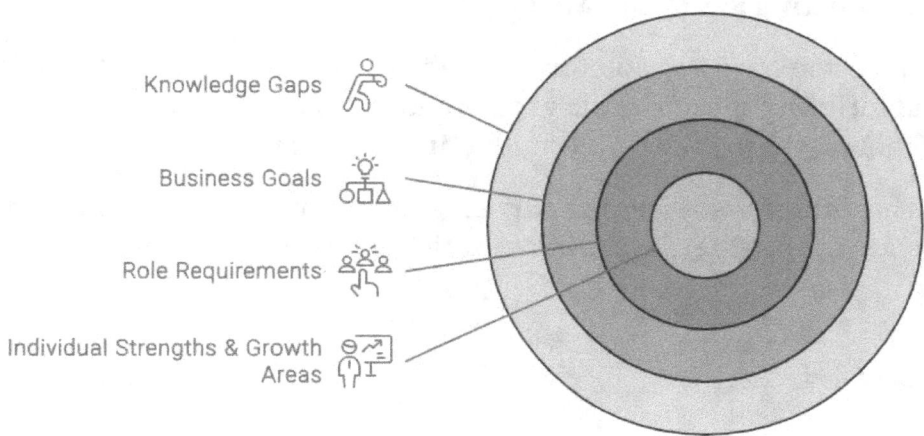

- **Individual strengths & growth areas** - What is each person already great at versus skills they need to improve? Personal assessments and manager feedback reveal development needs.

- **Role requirements** - What competencies does excellence in each job role require? Job analysis identifies must-have abilities.

- **Business goals** - What capabilities will drive key results and strategy execution based on your plans? Align training to bridge this gap.

- **Knowledge gaps** - In which topics do teams need deeper expertise based on challenges faced? Prioritize training to address these.

Precision is paramount. While generalized courses help build a broad base, targeted learning goes the extra mile to tailor training to the individual's and organization's needs for maximum payoff.

With specific needs identified, you can tailor development plans. Targeted learning has a large ROI because it efficiently addresses needs.

Conducting Skills Gap Analysis

Once you have a vision for targeted development, the next step is identifying specific skills gaps to address. The best way to shine a light on these needs is by conducting skills gap analysis.

This process analyzes the current state versus the required future state across three levels: organizational, team, and individual.

Gathering Data

- **Organizational analysis** - Review strategic plans to identify capabilities critical for future success. Compare to current state.

- **Team analysis** - Assess skills needed for optimal performance based on goals and challenges teams face in their function.

- **Individual analysis** - Collect input on strengths and weaknesses through assessments, self-evaluations, peer feedback, and manager input during performance reviews.

Cast a wide net through quantitative competency assessments and qualitative feedback. Multiple data points provide an accurate picture.

Spotting Priority Gaps

- Look for patterns in the organizational and team-level data to reveal capability gaps shared across groups. Address common needs through broad training.

- Note recurring themes in individual data to pinpoint strengths to leverage and high priority weakness areas to improve across the workforce.

Personalizing Development

- Based on insights gathered, tailor training plans to each employee.

- For example, assign public speaking courses to individuals who need to improve presentation skills.

- Or develop a customer service training program for functions needing to boost these competencies.

Don't rely on assumptions. Take a data-driven approach to shape targeted development initiatives.

Development Opportunities

Once you pinpoint priority skills, choose how to build them. This is best done in a catalog. Development tactics include:

- **Training Programs**
Courses, workshops, certifications
- **Stretch Assignments**
Challenging projects to expand skills.
- **Coaching and Mentorship**
Guidance from experienced employees **Job Shadowing ** Observing other roles
- **Online Learning**
Webinars, tutorials, and courses

Enable growth through a blend of learning formats. Employees appreciate personalized opportunities tailored to their goals.

Tracking Progress

Targeted development is a strategic enablement approach, but how do you know your efforts are actually working?

It's crucial to measure progress through quantifiable metrics. Analytics concretely demonstrate training's ROI, helping justify investments.

Here are keyways to evaluate effectiveness:

Testing Knowledge Gains

- Administer exams before and after training to assess competency improvements.

For example, quiz sales reps on product knowledge before and after assigned eLearning courses.

Self-Assessments

- Have employees rate their confidence levels in skills before and after training on a numeric scale.

Ask software engineers to self-assess coding expertise before and after a coding bootcamp.

Manager Feedback

- Gather manager perspectives on skill levels before and after training through surveys or meetings.

Poll project manager's managers on leadership capabilities before and after a management workshop.

Work Quality Analysis

- Review work samples before and after training to evaluate improvements.

Compare financial models created before and after an Excel training to identify increased sophistication.

Measure across qualitative and quantitative metrics for a holistic view. Proving progress builds support for enablement investments.

The journey continues! Focusing enablement initiatives on priority skills accelerates growth. Onward!

CHAPTER 6 - MANAGER COACHING

We've explored broad training, hands-on practice, and targeted development. Now let's look at manager coaching tactics to further grow talent.

Managers have an invaluable opportunity to mentor employees. Their guidance and feedback help unlock potential.

The Role of Managers

Enablement extends beyond formal training. Managers should:

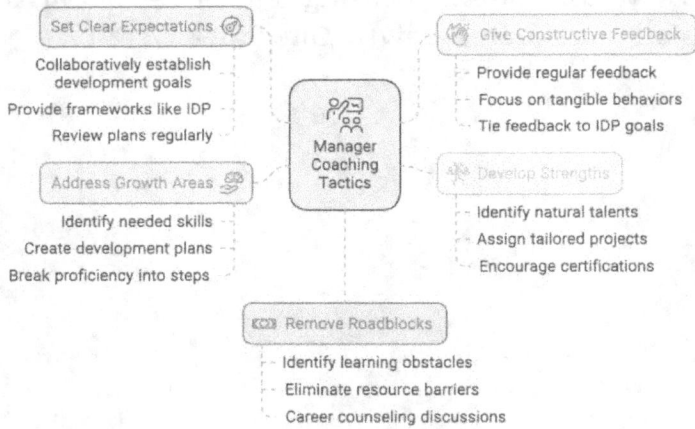

Set Clear Expectations

- Collaboratively establish development goals aligned to business objectives and career aspirations. This gives employees direction and purpose.

- Provide frameworks like IDP (Individual Development Plans) to define incremental objectives. Review plans regularly.

Give Constructive Feedback

- Don't just give annual performance reviews. Provide regular feedback so employees can course correct.

- Focus commentary on tangible behaviors vs. personality critique. Be specific yet kind.

- Tie feedback to progress on IDP goals. Recognize achievements.

Develop Strengths

- Help employees identify natural talents and strengths. Look for ways to activate these in their role.

- Assign projects tailored to their capabilities to build confidence and passions.

- Encourage pursuing certifications or education expanding strengths.

Address Growth Areas

- Work together to identify skills employees need to develop through training or on-the-job practice. Create plans to level up.

- Recognize growth areas take time and support. Break proficiency into achievable steps.

Remove Roadblocks

- Some obstacles block learning, like lack of time, access, or resources. Help identify and eliminate these hurdles.

- If the employee is demotivated, have career counseling discussions to reconnect to purpose.

With managers actively invested in enablement, employees have a trusted advocate for their professional journey.

Cultivating Impactful Coaching Skills in Managers

In the last section, we discussed the manager's pivotal enablement role. But effective coaching requires developing key skills. Mentorship excellence isn't automatic.

Let's explore core competencies to cultivate in managers through training:

Active Listening

- Give full attention when employees are speaking. Avoid distractions and multitasking.

- Use open body language and make eye contact to show engagement.

- Paraphrase what you hear and ask clarifying questions to understand thoroughly.

Asking Powerful Questions

- Ask open-ended questions that spark introspection and problem solving vs. yes/no questions.

- Follow the 5 Why's approach to dig to the root of challenges. Keep asking "why?" to unearth deeper issues.

- Inquire about goals, strengths, growth areas. Draw out their thinking.

Constructive Feedback

- Frame feedback to be caring yet candid. Focus on behaviors not the person.

- Give frequent real-time feedback so details are fresh. Don't just review annually.

- Ensure feedback is specific, measurable, and actionable. Explain clearly how to improve.

S.M.A.R.T. Goal Setting

- Make development goals specific, measurable, achievable, relevant, and time bound.

- Collaborate to define incremental objectives that ladder up to growth and business aims.

Developmental Assignments

- Know each person's strengths and passions. Assign projects allowing them to expand in these areas.

- Make connections for learning opportunities like cross-training, mentors, and courses.

Dedicate time to build these skills through workshops. Coach managers to become great coaches unlocking their team's potential. It takes one to grow one!

Making Coaching a Daily Habit

Like any new skill, coaching abilities require practice to stick. Don't let your manager training be a one-time event. Instead instill coaching as a daily habit.

Weave mentoring touchpoints into regular management rhythms:

Weekly Check-ins

- Have brief stand up meetings to discuss:
    - Current projects and pending work.
    - Where they may be stuck and need support
    - Recent wins to celebrate.
- Keep chats casual and conversational. Foster trust through routine cadence.

Quarterly Performance Reviews

- Do formal, thorough reviews of:
    - Progress on development goals
    - Achievements and growth areas
    - Updated IDP objectives
- Make time for rich dialogue and next step planning.

Monthly Personal Development Plan Reviews

- Revisit documented learning objectives and adjust based on recent feedback and insights.
- Discuss progress on training and assignments. Identify additional resources needed.

Pulse Surveys

- Gauge engagement through light monthly or quarterly surveys.

- Assess satisfaction with growth opportunities, manager support, and other enablement.

Don't let coaching be an occasional event - make it a habit! Like daily exercise, frequent mentoring interactions compound abilities over time.

Through perpetual feedback loops, enablement becomes woven into management DNA. Employees will embrace a coach's guidance on this never-ending journey.

Onward! Next, we will explore measuring enablement success.

CHAPTER 7 – QUANTIFYING THE JOURNEY

After implementing the four stages of the Enablement Skill Stack, it's crucial to analyze your initiative's impact.

Measurement provides priceless insights into what's working, what's not, and how to improve. As Peter Drucker said, "What gets measured gets managed."

Let's explore key areas to quantify success:

Participation Rates

Track program enrollment, attendance, completion percentages, and hours spent training per employee. High participation indicates people are engaged in development opportunities.

Set clear goals around minimum training hours expected by role and monitor progress. Encourage universal involvement through incentives and recognition.

Knowledge and Skill Gains

Assess competency improvements through testing and self-evaluations before and after training. Gather manager feedback on applied skills.

Schedule regular skill assessments to benchmark progress. Share results to showcase growth and motivate continuous improvement.

Employee Perceptions

Survey satisfaction ratings, willingness to recommend programs, and qualitative feedback. Hold focus groups to hear experiences firsthand.

Solicit input at multiple points: right after training, a few months later, and in annual engagement surveys. Uncover evolving needs.

Business Impact

Connect development initiatives to improved performance metrics. Assess productivity gains, quality improvements, and cost savings from new skills and processes.

Align learning goals to specific business objectives from the start. Track quantitative results over time to prove financial returns.

Retention and Engagement

Analyze turnover rates, promotion velocity, and employee loyalty between trained and untrained groups. Study links between programs and satisfaction.

Retention savings alone often outweigh training costs. Tout these benefits to showcase enablement's strategic value.

Apply both quantitative and qualitative measures for a holistic picture. Let the data guide decisions to maximize training ROI and progress. The journey continues as we constantly improve!

CHAPTER 8 - SUSTAINING GROWTH

We've now explored the four steps of the Enablement Skill Stack in depth. In this chapter, let's discuss how to make your learning culture stick.

Sustaining an enablement mindset takes work - but the effort pays off manifold in employee satisfaction, innovation, and performance.

Make It Part of Your Identity

Stellar companies like Google, Netflix, and LinkedIn have become synonymous with talent development. Enablement is core to their employer brand.

- Promote learning internally and externally as central to your culture. Feature coaching, training completion, and employee features centrally in emails, events, and communications.

- Tie enablement to company values. For example, EY's value of "continuous learning" underpins their focus on development.

- Make enablement part of your leadership principles. Amazon lists "Has a Passion for Development" as a key tenet for managers.

When something becomes integral to who you are, you're motivated to maintain it.

Stay Agile

Your organization's needs will evolve, so enablement efforts must as well.

- Keep training targeted by re-evaluating skills gaps and business goals annually. Refresh programs to address emerging needs.

- Routinely seek employee feedback through pulse surveys, focus groups, or learning committees. Ask what additional development would help performance.

- Observe trends in corporate learning, like microlearning, gamification, and virtual reality. Incorporate cutting-edge methods.

By keeping a finger on the pulse, your programs stay highly relevant to current objectives.

Celebrate and Inspire

Spotlight enablement wins to keep momentum going.

- Praise training completion, certifications earned, skills demonstrated. Make successes visible through newsletters, calls, and internal social networks.

- Publicize promotions and achievements of program participants. Tie learning to career advancement.

- Share inspiring participant testimonials. Storytelling sparks passion.

Maintain excitement by making learning achievements highly visible.

Keep Building the Stack

The Skill Stack doesn't end after four steps. Continue adding enabling elements:

- **Leadership training** - Develop manager coaching abilities.

- **Stretch assignments** - Provide challenging rotational assignments.

- **New mentors** - Pair employees with mentors outside their department.

- **Learning hackathons** - Host ideation sessions for new enablement approaches.

Commit to constant improvement. Evolve programs, tools, and methods to take development to the next level.

By making enablement an integral part of your culture, your future-proof your workforce. They will rise to meet whatever the future brings!

Onward and upward - always!

CHAPTER 9 – BEYOND TACTICS: THE CULTURAL FOUNDATIONS OF ENABLEMENT

So far, we've explored the tactical steps involved in enablement, from assessments to customized training and tools. But truly transforming an organization requires looking beyond skills to mindsets.

Even the most well-crafted enablement program will flounder without the right cultural soil to take root in. Psychological and emotional elements provide the fertile conditions for people to blossom.

Let's dig into key intangibles for empowering human potential:

Cultivating Growth Mindsets for Enablement

The foundation of continuous learning is believing abilities can be developed, not fixed at birth. Employees with rigid "fixed mindsets" see little point in trying to improve skills. They view talents as innate and unchangeable.

Conversely, those with "growth mindsets" recognize skills like creativity and leadership can be strengthened over time through dedication and practice. They are more receptive to enablement initiatives.

Some ways to nurture growth mindsets:

Praise Effort, Not Inborn "Talent"

Managers should recognize hard work, perseverance, and the process - not just the end result. This reinforces that progress comes through effort.

For example, acknowledge an employee's grit for presenting 10 drafts before mastering a deck rather than just applauding their inherent skills.

Model Being a Learner

Leaders should openly discuss their own growth journeys, knowledge gaps, and development goals. This demonstrates being a lifelong learner.

When an executive discusses how a management course helped them become a better mentor, it powerfully signals that seeking growth is important at all levels.

Challenge Limiting Beliefs

Help employees notice self-limiting beliefs like "I'm too old to learn new technology" that become self-fulfilling prophecies. Assuring people of their potential to grow is empowering.

When a rigid perspective prevents someone from believing new abilities can be built, have an open dialogue to widen their self-perception.

With the right culture of malleable skills, enablement can truly take root and help people maximize their potential.

Making Learning Central to Employees' Identities

For enablement to truly take hold, learning needs to become an integral part of employees' self-identity - not just another task. When people see enrichment as part of who they are, motivation follows.

Ways to cultivate learning as a core value:

Spotlight Learning Role Models

Recognize employees who exemplify a passion for continuous growth. Their stories inspire others to take ownership of self-enablement.

For example, interview digital skills masters willing to teach colleagues about new technologies. Their love of learning is infectious.

Celebrate Enrichment Milestones

Praise steps like completing training courses, earning certifications, teaching workshops. Make achievements highly visible through newsletters, calls, social media.

Publicly congratulate an employee who completes a technical bootcamp. This makes learning something to aspire towards.

Integrate Learning into Performance

Include continuous growth in job expectations and reviews. This makes enrichment not just a box to check but central to roles.

Managers could set goals around knowledge sharing, completing X training hours, or teaching seminars.

Institutionalize Reflection

Ask teams to summarize "lessons learned" after major initiatives. This reflective practice cements insights for the future.

Reserve the last 5 minutes of meetings to capture key learnings. This habit fuels improvement.

When learning becomes entwined with people's sense of identity, enrichment becomes self-propelling rather than a chore. Choose people who share this intrinsic drive for growth.

Harnessing Brain Science for Enablement

Emerging insights from neuroscience and psychology offer lessons for empowering learning in the workforce:

Repeat Concepts over Time

Rather than cramming training into a single session, revisiting key ideas over spaced intervals aids deeper retention as neural pathways solidify.

For example, refresh employees on brand values quarterly rather than just at onboarding. Repetition across months ingrains knowledge.

Tap into Social Learning

The brain remembers better when learning is an interactive social experience rather than passive lecture. Mirror neurons activate when we feel connected to others.

Enable group discussions, peer feedback, and games tapping into our wired-in social nature.

Let People Discover

Having learners actively figure out concepts through experimentation and problem-solving encodes deeper understanding compared to just hearing information.

Pose challenges like case studies for groups to work through versus traditional presentations. Self-discovery sticks.

Understanding these mental patterns allows us to architect enablement initiatives leveraging how our brains are naturally wired to acquire new skills and knowledge. The mind is an endless frontier!

Blending neuroscience, psychology, and culture creates an environment where enablement reaches its full potential. Let's continue exploring additional dimensions beyond tactical considerations. The journey has endless horizons for us to reach new heights!

CHAPTER 10 - LEADING THE CHANGE TO SKILL STACK ENABLEMENT

The Enablement Skill Stack offers a powerful model for developing talent. But evolving from traditional programs requires change management finesse.

Even if current methods are flawed, the familiar still feels comfortable. Shifting mindsets and workflows takes sensitivity.

Let's explore steps to thoughtfully transition to the Skill Stack:

Making the Case for Change

Transition starts with illustrating current state limitations and contrasting the possibilities. Data often resonates more than words alone.

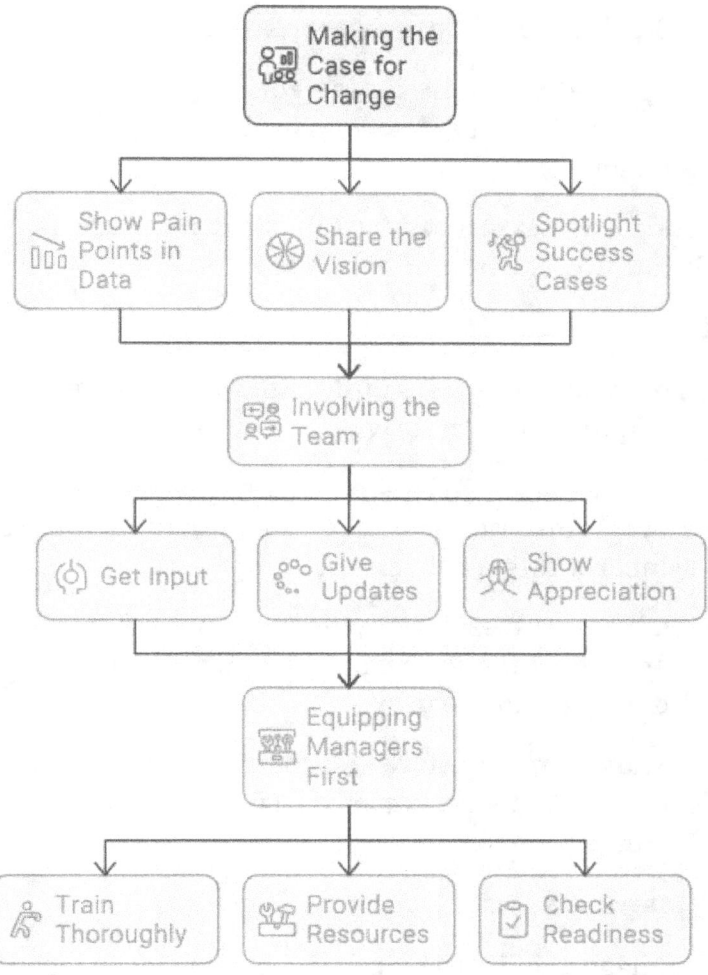

- **Show pain points in data** - Present metrics on low engagement, stagnant skills, poor retention under status quo. Numbers tell the story.

- **Share the vision** - Paint a picture of what extraordinary enablement could look like with Skill

Stack adopted. Inspire people with potential.

- **Spotlight success cases** - Point to companies already using the model successfully. Social proof builds belief.

With a compelling reason why established methods fall short, people unite around the need for change.

Involving the Team

People support what they help build. Engage employees early as partners in shaping the path forward.

- **Get input** - Ask about pain points with current programs and ideas for the future model. Listen and incorporate feedback.

- **Give updates** - Provide regular progress reports and continue gathering insights. Transparency and dialogue build trust.

- **Show appreciation** - Recognize contributions with thanks and small rewards. People support what they create.

Equipping Managers First

Frontline managers will make or break adoption success. Give them tools to become skillful change champions.

- **Train thoroughly** - Ensure managers deeply understand the new model and rationale. Address concerns in open forums.

- **Provide resources** - Equip managers to answer team questions and troubleshoot hurdles.

- **Check readiness** - Assess manager confidence levels regularly. They are your enablement of enablement.

Here is a detailed change plan to move to the Skill Stack framework, including impacted systems and artifacts:

Skill Stack Transition Plan

1. Formulate Target State Vision

- Document ideal Enablement Skill Stack model for our organization including all components and flows.

- Create guiding principles to shape rollout.

2. Impact Assessment

- Identify key stakeholders across L&D, HR, IT, managers, employees.

- Analyze current systems and processes that will be impacted:
    - LMS system
    - Onboarding curriculum
    - Performance management templates
    - Development plans

3. Build Cross-Functional Team

- Recruit project team with representatives across departments like L&D, HR, IT, Change Management

- Align on roles, responsibilities, and optimal collaboration processes.

4. Create Transition Roadmap

- Define project phases with timeline spanning ~6 months:
    - Draft framework
    - Stakeholder input

- Systems integration
- Manager training
- Employee communication
- Pilot launch
- Iterative improvements

5. Design Enablement Architecture

- Map new workflows, systems, templates, assessments, content formats, and touchpoints required to bring Skill Stack to life.

Artifacts:

- Skill assessment templates
- Individual development plan templates
- Updated performance review formats
- New learning paths in LMS
- Change communications.
- Stakeholder analysis
- Manager training curriculum

6. Engineer Required Capabilities

- Configure LMS to support new learning pathways.
- Develop rating systems for skill assessments.
- Build templates for IDPs and reviews.
- Create pilot participant criteria.

7. Equip Change Agents

- Create guiding coalition from managers to set example.

- Provide in-depth training on model, rationale, and leading change.

8. Communicate for Awareness & Excitement

- Multi-channel employee communications campaign before, during, after launch.

9. Launch Pilot, Iterate, and Scale Gradually

- Start with pilot group, gather feedback, improve based on learnings.

- Expand to additional teams in multiple waves to smooth adoption.

- Maintain consistent messaging and celebrate wins.

10. Institutionalize Continuous Improvement

- Build measurement mechanisms and feedback channels.

- Communicate updates and involve teams in shaping enhancements.

- Celebrate employee impact stories.

CHAPTER 11 – FINAL REFLECTIONS

W e've now reached the summit after an intensive journey of learning and growth. Let's spend this concluding chapter reflecting on key takeaways and looking ahead.

The Path We've Traveled

Through these pages, we've explored:

- Why continuous enablement creates standout teams.

- How to instill learning into your culture

- The four steps of the Enablement Skill Stack

- Tactics to sustain skills and passion.

I hope this guide provided a strategic yet practical roadmap. My aim was to empower you to cultivate an empowered, future-ready workforce.

Key Takeaways

- Enablement Starts from the Top
- Leaders must role model continuous learning to set the culture. Management's engagement is essential.
- Blend Formal and Informal Learning
- Leverage a mix of structured training with peer sharing, coaching, stretch assignments, and experiential learning.
- Target Development to Needs
- Tailor enablement to employee strengths, weaknesses, and business objectives for high ROI.
- Empower Self-Directed Learning
- Provide resources for people to guide their own growth while leading overall strategy.
- Recognize and Celebrate Growth
- Highlight achievements and promotions to reinforce learning's links with success.

These tenets will serve you well on your journey. Feel free to flip back and remind yourself as needed!

Your Path Ahead

Now it's time to chart your organization's unique course. What is your enablement vision? How will you reimagine possibilities for your people?

Begin by defining your "True North." Clarify the skills and knowledge that will set your team apart. Then bring passion and perseverance as you take the first steps.

Remember - the climb makes us stronger. Through challenge we reach new heights. Enablement is a lifelong journey of discovery, not just a project with an end date.

I'll leave you with this final thought: *The people are the power.* If you invest in their growth, they will drive your success as leaders and as an organization.

I wish you the very best as you architect your people-first future. Go boldly and lead wisely. The view is beautiful from the top!

Onward and upward, always.

CHAPTER 12 – USEFUL TEMPLATES

ACCELERATING YOUR ENABLEMENT JOURNEY WITH TEMPLATES

W e've now explored the fundamentals of building an empowered workforce through the four stages of the Enablement Skill Stack. But what good is a roadmap without some wheels to gain momentum?

In this chapter, I've curated a collection of templates and tools to help kickstart your learning programs. Consider these a gift basket to get you rolling faster down the path of enablement.

Building a learning organization takes work, but you don't have to reinvent the wheel. These resources aim to save you time and energy as you architect your workforce of the future.

Like a new cook trying complex recipes, it helps to start with some basic ingredients prepped. You can still add your own special spins and adjustments. My goal is to provide a head start, not constrain your creativity.

Let's briefly overview the templates provided:

Individual Development Plans Outline personalized learning journeys for team members.

Skills Gap Analyses Reveal areas to target for improvement.

Coaching Meeting Frameworks Enable effective mentoring conversations.

Training Feedback Surveys Gather input to improve programs.

And more covering mentorship, onboarding, assessments, and communications.

The specifics will evolve as you tailor to your culture and objectives. Consider these starting points you can make your own.

May these tools give your enablement engine a little more horsepower. Floor it! I'm excited to see your unique Enablement Skill Stack creations accelerate success.

Now let's get to the templates...

Individual Development Plan Template

- Employee Name
- Manager Name
- Current Role & Main Responsibilities
- Long Term Career Goals (3-5 years)
- Short Term Goals for This Year
  - Goal 1: Improve presentation skills.
    - Actions: Complete public speaking course, practice monthly team presentations
  - Goal 2: Expand financial analysis skills.
    - Actions: Shadow finance manager, take Excel modeling course, review case studies
- Key Development Areas to Build
  - Public speaking
  - Financial modeling
  - Cross-functional collaboration

- Planned Training & Growth Experiences
  - Public speaking for leaders' course (Q2)
  - Excel modeling certification (Q3)
  - Finance manager job shadow (Q4)
  - Lead book club on influencer skills (Q3-Q4)
- Target Dates for Completion
  - Public speaking course: 6/30
  - Job shadow: 11/30
  - Book club: Ongoing
- Quarterly Status Updates & Progress Notes
  - Q1: Discussed opportunities with finance manager.
  - Q2: Completed public speaking course; gave presentation at all-hands meeting.
  - Q3: Halfway through Excel course; led first book club meeting.

Skills Gap Analysis Template

- Role: Customer Service Representative
- Required Competencies:
  - Product knowledge
  - Customer empathy
  - Active listening
  - Issue resolution
  - Documentation skills
- Individual's Self-Assessed Skill Level
  - Product knowledge: Proficient
  - Empathy: Intermediate
  - Active listening: Beginner
  - Issue resolution: Intermediate
  - Documentation: Beginner
- Manager Assessment of Skills
  - Product knowledge: Proficient
  - Empathy: Beginner
  - Active listening: Beginner
  - Issue resolution: Intermediate
  - Documentation: Beginner
- Gap Analysis Results
  - Empathy, active listening, and documentation identified as gaps.
- Priority Gaps to Address
  - Active listening
  - Documentation
- Recommended Training
  - Active listening workshop

- Documentation processes course

Manager Coaching Meeting Agenda

- Progress on Goals
    - What progress has been made on development goals?

    - What's going well and what's challenging?

- Current Projects
    - Brief updates on key projects and initiatives

- Resources Needed
    - What support or resources would be helpful?

- Constructive Feedback
    - Provide 1-2 pieces of constructive developmental feedback.

- Recognition
    - What recent wins or achievements deserve acknowledgment?

- Next Steps
    - Summarize action items and next steps.

Training Session Feedback Survey

- On a scale of 1-5, how relevant was this training to your development needs?

- On a scale of 1-5, how engaging and effective was the facilitator?

- What were the 2-3 biggest takeaways for you?

- What could be improved about the content or delivery?

- How likely are you to apply what you learned?

- Would you recommend this training to others on your team? Why or why not?

Mentor Program Kickoff Checklist

- Define program objectives.

- Outline mentor selection criteria

- Develop mentor training curriculum.

- Host mentor orientation session

- Establish mentee application process.

- Review applications and match mentors to mentees

- Send match notifications and introduce paired groups.

- Provide mentor/mentee training resources.

- Schedule check-ins at 3 months, 6 months, and 12 months

New Manager Assimilation Plan

- Assign mentor outside immediate team.
- Schedule job shadowing with other managers.
- Complete conflict management workshop
- Participate in new leaders' cohort meetings.
- Lead project to expand cross-functional exposure.
- Connect with other new managers for peer learning.
- Take unconscious bias and coaching skills training.
- Set goals for skill development focus areas.

Learning Resource Library Wishlist

- Books
  - Crucial Conversations, The Coaching Habit, Radical Candor
- Online Courses
  - Conflict management, strategic thinking, mentorship
- Videos
  - TED talks on building trust and influence.
- Podcasts
  - Managing teams, effective communications
- Webinars
  - Unconscious bias, sparking creativity.
- Simulations
  - Strategic decision making, public speaking.

Manager Coaching Session Guide

- Progress on Goals
    - What progress have you made on your development goals this month?

    - What successes are you proud of?

    - What has been challenging? Where are you stuck?

- Current Work Projects
    - Give me a brief update on your top 3 priorities and projects right now.

    - Do you need any support or resources to move them forward?

- Constructive Feedback
    - I wanted to discuss your presentation last week. You had strong content but seemed nervous. Let's role play to help build your public speaking confidence.

    - Going forward, be sure to send me status updates on the client project every Friday. Timeliness is an area where we can improve.

- Recognition
    - You did a great job stepping up to lead the community service event. Your commitment to getting involved beyond your core role is impressive.

- Development Plans
    - Now that you've completed the Excel course, how can we build on that to expand your data analysis skills?

    - I'd like to see you shadow the marketing team to increase cross-functional knowledge. I'll connect you with their manager.

- Additional Support
  - Do you feel you are getting enough coaching and resources from me? How can I better support you?

New Hire Onboarding Checklist

- ❑ Assign mentor

- ❑ Send welcome gift

- ❑ Tour office and intro to team

- ❑ Review organization chart and role overview

- ❑ Complete HR paperwork

- ❑ Set up technology access

- ❑ Review company policies and procedures

- ❑ Schedule first week check-ins

- ❑ Discuss skill development goals

- ❑ Take introductory compliance courses

- ❑ Shadow top performer

- ❑ Set day goals

- ❑ Check in on progress and feedback

Skill Development Goal Planning

- Current Role & Responsibilities

- Key Skills Needed for Success
  - Communication, leadership, collaboration, etc.

- My Strengths
  - What skills do you excel at currently?

- Potential Growth Areas
  - What skills would help you grow and succeed?

- Goals for Skill Development
  - Public speaking, strategic thinking, influencing, etc.

- Action Plan
  - Training programs, job shadowing, coaching, books, etc.

- Target Timeframes

- Progress Milestones

Training Program Post-Mortem

- Program Name & Description

- Number of Participants

- Program Goals
  - What skills/knowledge did we aim to build?

- Metrics to Evaluate
  - Completion rates, engagement, improvement in skills, business impact

- Successes
  - What worked well?

- Areas for Improvement
  - What can be improved next time?

- Key Learnings & Recommendations
  - Summarize takeaways to inform future programs.

Mentorship Kickoff Meeting Agenda

- Discuss mentee's background and goals.

- Establish guidelines for the relationship.

- Outline expectations around communication cadence

- Identify development areas to focus mentoring.

- Set agenda for meetings.

- Discuss opportunities for job shadowing or meetings.

- Provide mentee with resources like books, videos, courses.

- Schedule consistent check-in meetings

- Determine metrics to measure success.

- Share contact information for ongoing communication.

Quarterly Training Recap Email to Employees

- Courses Completed (totals and highlights)
- Certificates Earned
- Current Popular Pathways/Courses
- New Courses Coming Next Quarter
- Recognition Highlights (power user, most improved, etc.)
- Participant Testimonials
- Reminder on Development Goals
- Resources for Self-Directed Learning

Notes

Notes

Notes

Notes

Notes

Notes

Notes

Notes